Bunch
of
Animals

Cloudbank Books
Corvallis, Oregon

Also by Henry Hughes

Poetry
Men Holding Eggs
Moist Meridian
Shutter Lines

Nonfiction
Back Seat with Fish

Edited Collections
Art of Angling: Poems about Fishing
Fishing Stories

Bunch

of

Animals

Henry Hughes

ISBN (hardcover) 978-0-9824867-4-0
ISBN (softcover) 978-0-9824867-3-3

Cover art by Gregory Poulin.
Cover design by Natalia Bueno.

Cloudbank Books
215 SW Madison Ave,
Corvallis, OR 97333

1 2 3 4 5 6 7 8 9 0

for Chloë
close in the cold night

Contents

IV Earning Some Blue

V At Any Cost

VI What's Left

VII The Last Tool You'll Need

I

Dollar in the Sand

Eccentric Sand Dollar

If you're poor and weird,
the failed test of a purple urchin,
washed-up, stinking, flitting flies,
don't expect much respect,

but with money or a brand,
craft coin kitsch from a mermaid's purse,
then you're eccentric —
a dollar in the sand,

in the seaside shop, on the window sill,
bleached clean
for the tourists,
faintly impressed with a star or flower
from an earlier, richer,
better life.

Doctor Doolittle

What musical of bold silly
from the little wild world inside
still chirps and howls out
to creatures suddenly unstranged?

Top hat, waistcoat,
fish bubbling, pig knuckling —
always that dogged defense of diversity,
always singing-up for animals,
even when England scorned
those improper tongues of Irish setter
and American skunk. The spicy roar of tiger.

I, too, practice queer quacking,
then caterwaul to grammar girls sipping tea,
kinked-tailed mouse paging
my crummy pocket
when a horse coughs reception
clear. *Easy*, I nicker and whinny,

prescribing apple lozenges
and more ridiculous verse
for this fever of cultivation.

Least Sandpiper

Least, maybe,
but a whole flock is a big idea, turning tight
to whim and weather
and the delicious
green rind
of the bay.
Probe and pick, peep and eat,
they alight beside
us mucky clammers
shucked by the soft company.
Then up-flock —
white bellies, black backs, white, black, white —
like so much, so quickly
in
and out
of our lives.

Ice Plant Foreman

His whole life on ice,
three hundred tons a day, silver cube,
blue block,
flake and plate—a plant foreman
never too late or cold to smile
or hug his daughters, even
when August melted his nerves,
and his wife went dry. Every day
more complaints, inspections, breakdowns—
everyone knew he wasn't sick
when he called in. Summer trout
down deep, but catchable. A mountain of water
behind a dam
might tell a man
there will always be enough
of himself
if he manages time and flow,
the lake's hot shimmer,
wide brimmed on a slow troll.
Ice in the cooler for keepers.

Rock Wallabies

Because of their isolation, many colonies
of wallabies are going extinct
       —Sydney Morning Herald

At dusk
I kill the truck
and scan the craggy caves
of magnetic stone
where the last rock wallabies wake alone,
long-faced and lapping the drying pool of their genes.
A young buck noses the scree—
he's a rock islander like me,
miles from other families,
avoiding foxes,
sun shy and night hungry.
I keep saying
goat farming with my dad
is enough, but every week
I drive the dusty road to town,
get drunk and thump around—
a load of seed
to launch and drown.

How I Became a Country Musician

She'd draw all the stares,
farm-raised and spangle born,
asked out by a twice-her-age
with grain too rich for doves.

What a swirl
at the town pool. How boys goggled
to see her dive. Why everyone
said *Hot,* when the water
was just right.

I wanted her hips in my saddle,
her voice on my neck.
But she had no lips for a hound-rounder,
a rough-tongued boy
in cracked boots.

So I worked
like nobody's business. Traded shooting
for strumming
in my damp basement room.

One June night at a friend's house
she sat with me and listened.
Rocking perfect time, eyes in mine,
she started softly singing.

Like Eels

in
lotioned
ooze
and mossy
caves,
tasting, touching,
swallowing
what hauls them
to the light,
cream-bellied
and turned to bite,
then skinned,
slit and spun
firm and oily
over the grill's loom,
brushed sweet
and salty
for us to eat,
discuss
if we must,
but mostly
trust,
making sense
or love
that's real —
before
we slip away
again
like eels

That Woman Across the Street,

she's let herself go.
Gray faced in stained sweats,
flip-flopping
to Circle K for cigarettes and pop.
No one mows the grass, rakes the rot,
or visits. The window's yellow light
burning late
into early. Maybe she's sick, depressed.
Age blowing her mind into ash.
I don't know. What can I do?
We never got close. Never talked much
after those first weeks
she was so excited
about planting a new apple tree
and her troubled son
who had just joined the army.

Action

He's big, he's mean, and he kills a lot of bad guys.
No one cared that he was gay.
> —testimony from a Pentagon report

More than grunts,
we tongue Pashto and Arabic
in the dusty streets and shops. Watching, listening
carefully—very carefully—between
straight black abayas and embroidered white caps.
We'd rather talk them down, but we'll shoot.
We know the soft and hard of man. Face in the tower,
bulge in the pants. Our M-16s and that nasty SAW
put the *queer fear* in their Sharia law.
Like Blacks marching on the old South,
we're a nightmare bayonet up their hanging moons.
Don't get fucking captured, I tell my men, and they don't.
Snugging green belts across our tight abs,
we smarten our collars
and slip on those big blonde boots. Fit in? Come on,
we're good at that. We had to be.
Give us some action
and we can all relax.

II

Living with You

Aubade

Waking
under awning rain,
work-worried, debt-dark,
rubbing legs, pressing
  mouths unsweetened —
    kiss, kissing, sliding down,
      rising over, rock & kern, cresting
        into a gray day
          no longer
          possibly
          so bad.

Chorus Stegosaurus

The children sing
below the armored arch
of the museum's spike-tailed stegosaurus
guarding her silent young.

Their thin voices
a pocket of piping voles
waiting out the big Jurassic,
the rain of applause,
charming a few thousand dollars
for the remodel.

It's amazing what a singing child
and a couple cocktails
will do to a parent
after so much already raised, given and lost,
so much tucked-in, forgotten and dug-up,
footprints and lost teeth,
love and wonder
year after year.

Our boy laughs with the others
and runs over for a hug.
What are we doing now? he asks.
Whatever you want, we say,
knowing full well there are meteors, volcanoes,
steaming oceans and cities of smoke
choking our promises.

Cleaning the Lake Trout

I called my wife from the dock,
told her about the huge fish,
said I'd be staying another night.
Silence. Then *Okay, bye.*

Knifing through those rolls of pink fat,
I found a belly of bleached rainbows —
one so whole and fresh, I cleaned it, too,
rinsing out the green smear of PowerBait.
Heart, kidneys, liver.
A fist of orange eggs
thrown in the trash.

Alone in bed,
owls and crickets through cabin screens,
I read that lake trout
can reach my age, forty-five,
swimming alone
until those autumn nights
when they char
the cobbly dark
with their spawning fire.

Were We Sea Lions

The flowers said *Sorry.*

Days later I rinse the slimy vase,
push my hand down its glass throat,
rubbing kelpy ribbons of green haze
                              and hear a sea lion
calling so far from the sea —
that rubbery fat honk
of argue and bully,
bristle nose and body rub
as they get over the barnacled rocks
without the soft posy of apology,

just the wet and true,
as ugly as it sounds, my herring breath
and your scarred belly

belching all we've swallowed
about who's right and wrong,
getting to the belong
of sun and storm,
fat and warm
on this island together.

Taming

Curled in the warm valley of legs,
our cat sleeps, nudging early faces.
We rub his purring chin and tufted ears,
smile and talk gently with one another.

Some mornings I don't feel so good—
hungover, exhausted, alone or worse.
Paw, nuzzle, then a little bite
I shove away. But to him it's just a game
learned long ago,

when a man
shot a wildcat off a snowy limb, pulled out his arrow,
felt her plush striped weight,
followed her tracks to the dry cave,
feathers and bones, the crying kittens
gathered in soft leather.

If they survive the journey, he thought,
there's a woman who would love
to try what is said possible. He didn't imagine
she'd tame and break his heart,
over and over
for thousands of years.

Wood Ducks

Wary and red-eyed, they flew
from our canoe on the beaver pond,
and still enjoyed stardom.
Oh. Have you seen the wood ducks?
Another calendar and card. Another overrated,
illustrated, perfect pair of wood ducks. Until that
April morning my daughter and I spied the soft hen —
her gentle grays and browns, her Egyptian eyes,
the way she called to the high box in the alder.
One by one, a dozen day-olds dropped
twenty feet to the ground,
bouncing and scrambling for water.
For weeks they gleaned shore and shallows,
hunted by owl and pike,
until the small, single parent family
disappeared.

Mother and Son

In the backyard
behind grimy spokes
of his upturned bicycle
he sees her robed,
unfolding a lawnchair.
Everything okay? she asks.
Chain's off, he says,
eying greasy links,
hands browner and bigger
every day.
She eases her thickening hips
onto plastic
beside the buzzing thyme,
and closes her eyes.
He sets the chain
and rides through the gate.
Stay close, she calls
to where
he feels the fast turn
of himself.

Rabbit Way

Before work, Chloë lifts
her silver-gray rabbit from his hutch, his little heart
fast in her arms, his ears perked to every garden rustle,

wide-eyed to wing-shadow, sniff-twitching
the breeze and bloom of her blouse, his long furry feet

itching for purchase and push. Chloë cradles
him to his back, the warm cosset of her plush chest,

ears stroked into smooth canoes turned over in the sand
after a river of worry: car doors, barking, a raccoon

clawing up the cage.
Oh, sweet bunny, she says softly, easing his pulse,

feet trackless in air, his eyes slowly, slowly closing
until there's not a sound, scent, or shape

of what we call fear, as she saves him day after day
in her own way, a rabbit way, hugged close in the warm
burrow of a moment.

Aesop's Turkey

Three days after Thanksgiving,
we boiled the turkey into broth.
I carried the pan-hearsed carcass
out to a wormy compost,
and came back
to savory steaming,
music, white wine, a call from the kids —
everybody fine.

We ladled out two big bowls,
plucked bread from the oven,
sat and ate our *Oh,*
this is so good. This is divine,
talking and spooning —

                   then *Ouch,*
I bit my tongue and bled,
and you slurped up a long hair.
You're eating yourselves, gobbled a turkey,
bright in our dining room.
He'd been pecking through our mulch —
Tender, juicy—
and saw the back door open.

My God, I gasped.
Relax, the turkey clucked,
head cocked to the side, circling our table.

III

Bunch of Animals

Black Dragon Fish

Dancing a mile down
for an ocean score,
her luminous black skirt
unzips to lure
a toothless mate
who can't relate
or feed himself.

It's only his milt
she's after.

Nights and days dissolve
in cold obscurity.
Who cares or even knows
about this icy fanged fish
deep inside the dark planet
where life makes
its own light?

Tundra Swans

God-cream and cloud.
Black-webbed desire and angel-winged grace.
The last sad song of evening.
Oh, the weight they lift—kick-flapping their long takeoff
when dogs run barking to the bank.

Before Greece and America,
before art and myth,
a waterland tundra, a reed pillowed nest.
The fox-watching pair nudging their dingy cygnets
water-ward, tipping for celery and snails.
And when those young wings fill out,
it's south before the ice.

Time does a lot for beauty despite its reputation.
Hear that? my daughter says
as we sip coffee on the red deck
of an October morning.
She tilts her head like a woman, smiles,
and whispers *Swans.*
We always hear them
before their white letters write the sky.
Before we think of something more
to make of them.

Fire Cats

My wife rips cardboard
into long roars for the fire,
then narrows into a cat
down alleys and lush yards,
a back door, treats and strokes,
a neighbor's warm couch
and nuzzled whispers.
All I can do is call
from the woodpile, then go back
and feed the flames.

We've heard of Pickle,
plucked from a treetop
and trucked to the old firehouse
for some card playing with the boys.
And Teaser's red tom
who helped Cat Stevens hook the moon.
There are sports teams,
a Magic card, and at least one
Louisiana strip club — Firecats —
where long tails
turn tips.

Last year
our cat really ran fire
when the church torched
their rat infested field around the corner,
her pads sweating on the vet's
stainless steel table
as he painted the burns.
Good thing she's not a witch, the vet joked,
and my wife rubbed her ears
tufted like smoky spells.

Earwig

Earwigs can lay eggs in your brain.
Ridiculous myth, right?
But something itched under my cap,
laddered against that dormer,
wet paintbrush in hand,
when a dobbed-white earwig
wriggled
out of a crack.
Funny at first,
shaking its bright annoyance.
Then sad
in its enameled dying
outside the bedroom
where my teenage son
slept-off a Facebook hangover—
party pictures of his beer-soaked "girlfriend"
between couch cushions,
and the "friend"
who drove her home.

Unlike most insects,
earwigs care for their young,
I learn from Wikipedia at lunch,
then I climb back up beside his window
with a little sympathy
and a little disgust.
The long wet strokes
covering nicely.

Bunch of Animals

It wasn't the vicious dogs
rust-chained to truck tires,
torn cats under the filthy porch,
or skunks in their high grass,
but the way greasy kids screamed around it all,
clawing and kicking through hungry mornings,
sticky nights, and maybe a few weeks of school
before the expelled heat drove them home.
Hey asshole, they greeted strangers, underpants in a tree, piss
darkened fence, the mother hacking and calling over and over
so fucking loud and screechy
our own rawness rose, rubbed, and bled
off our minds. *What a bunch of animals,* we'd say,
satisfied once they were old enough to get fired,
knocked-up, arrested, beat to a pulp,
or, one of them, killed at 19 over a pack of Camels.
No one I knew felt sorry for them
except in the pathetic *They're still human beings* way.
We might've stuck with honesty:
Poor creatures, starved and dangerous
as any wounded wild animal
wandering the edge of town.

Oregon City Shad

To be current in all things,
deep-cheeked, toothless,
      nose to tail,
         bright
     up the river's
dark channels and sandy shallows —
osprey clawed, hook
     pulled
        silver
    and green-backed
through the ceiling's harsh economy.
             Or swimming on,
       long shadowed, shoulder spotted
    under the freeway
and paper mill canyon,
foam roaring white,
eggs and milt,
     fin-flopped
        dying —
   an oily yellow
      tumble,
sturgeon sucked
    or rot-washed
     away.
      Or on like the rest of us,
spent
    but still spending
      back to the sea,
while the tiny new millions
    tremble
      in every
        uncertain
   river.

On Sunday

On Sunday he zincs moss
sponging the shingles,
re-flashes rain
into the right gutter,
straightens and screws down
the storm-whacked weather vane,

then washes his hands and sits down
for a juicy roast lamb
and a sunny talk
with his tall wife and two sons.

The youngest boy mentions the bats
hanging in the attic
like *spoiled monsters,* and the father laughs.
The older boy explains, *They eat mosquitoes
and are good for the environment,*
and they nod.
His wife chews quietly, wipes her mouth,
then says, *They don't belong
in this house.* He bows
to his peas for guidance.

Squishing through blue guano,
he smells the cost of devotion,
and without a prayer
gases bats into leaf bags.
The fallen weight of darkness
sagging in the street.

Territory

Tracks, scratchings,
a missing goat or spring lamb.
Saw a cougar crossing the road, he tells the sheriff
as they stand around the half-eaten man.
Damn big cat, the logger who found him
growls like a hound.
You know, the wildlife agent squints—
*cougars are the smallest and shyest
of the world's big cats,
and they usually don't do this.*

Like heartbreak is the smallest
of the world's problems,
desire the shyest of its storms.
But it took him only an angry few seconds
to stab that young guy
pawing his wife in their bed.

                           And one dark hour
to drag him
through that draw, where knives and claws,
saws and jaws
sized up nicely.

Time enough
to piss
on his boot.

IV
Earning Some Blue

Sermon to the Stockbrokers

In the Year of Our Lord, 2010

He who has not sold a wavy mirage
to a parched and hapless follower
forsakes the holy warrant.
Listen, my snake bitcoin brethren
of forced air investigations:
shudder not yesterday's folly,
           speak only of green futures —
equities, stock yards stamping pound and margin.
      Take that nervous goat
to the tile slaughter and swirl the drain
with its clotting guilt. Now into the dusty ring
          we ride the mountain-backed bull,
fattened on seedy accounts
scrimped from bare barns.
And though he stumble and snort,
    he rouses.
         My word is my bond, banners blare.
    Short the stock. Hedge the long. Open their purses.
Old black cloud, hold thy curses —
unhinge not a word or tear
before this holy act
transacts.

Nails in the Driveway

Drawing nails
to the good will of his magnet
swung on a string
over our gravel driveway,

my grandfather
thought
it was all the tearing apart
in our house
that turned the nails
against us. Screeched out with a claw,
bent, tossed, ignored,
until someone cursed another flat tire.
But it was just a little time and money.
A lot worse things
going on in our lives.

You get 'em all? I asked grandpa
when I got home from school,
a quiet can of points between his legs.
We'll never know, he smiled,
and let me swing
the magnet
for a while.

Earning Some Blue

Port Jefferson, Summer, 1982

Backyards in droopy blue tents,
playing baseball and bobbling a bad hop,
late throws, stoned casts
for slack tide blues that wouldn't bite
and girls who would
with Boone's Farm and an old blanket
on the barnacled beach.

Faking chores around the house,
bringing the slumped fence to brief attention,
spilling blue paint, smoking a joint,
losing the lawnmower's loose linkage
high in high grass.

Get a job! my father yelled.
Finally hired, Hendrick's blue potato truck,
grinding gears toward too long lunches,
fuckin' around, playing spud in the barrel.
Someone ratted
and we never got paid.

Asking Dad for ten bucks —
the slow headshake, indeterminate,
exhaling, then digging out
his warped black wallet, upsetting
the pressed shamrock
and handing me a one-sided Monopoly
blue. *Here's fifty,* he said.
And then I knew.

Dockhands

Me and Pete always said we'd buy
an old yacht and fix her up,
and charter summers for the stars.
Then I'd finish my coffee,
rub the pup's ears,
turn on the hose
and scrub

salt, oil, seagull crap,
the sticky gunk from coolers.
Rotting planks replaced,
line around a cleat, *Watch your step*,
blistering heat and a two-buck tip,
Thank you, sir,

under buggy dock lights
pumping someone's shit.
Tow, recharge, provision. Another call
for fuel and ice.
The women say, *He's nice*,
about our old gray dog snoring.

Aunt Madeline

As told by Mrs. Cooper

Madeline was always
tan skirts and black eyes
pressing questions
we thought and didn't say.
Did we really give Indians blankets with smallpox
and buy Manhattan for $24?
"Well . . ." the history teacher stalled.

1948, Andrew Jackson High School, hallway posters
warned of public places, polio, kissing, and the flu.
Doors had transoms then,
and chalk boards were slate blue,
so we could hear Principal White click and brow:
"You should be proud of your country, Madeline."
At seventeen we were proud of victory, boyfriends,
and the size of our busts. Then we saw Madeline necking
with a Mohawk iron worker the color of rust.

And the next week,
half the school was fever and shakes.
We blamed Madeline, called her a hussy,
but she never missed a class
or kissed an ass
to win that city back.

Scrub Jay

No JV scrub,
no third-string runt or bush leaguer.
Iron bill and flaring tail make you — *Jree?*
How silly to type a bird call. *Jreee?* Some bird, alright —
pinning a fledgling sparrow to the neighbor's roof
      and tearing out its breast.
Still I love your azure rule —
uncrowned prince
of perch and glide,
eating whatever flies or strides,
plucking spiders off the porch.

Did the West run dry of names for you?
      Spiderhawk,
           Bluebold, Jree-Jay, Wisewing.

Ah, what do you care? —
shrieking over peanuts on the picnic table, scaring
      starlings, strafing a cat,
a few more yards to go.

What Would You Do?

Yellow jackets stinging
from their crushed hole, snakes biting
a boot, the cat that scratched
the drunk guest who pulled his tail.
          But what would you do?
That dog we read about —
chewing through the walls of a cruel house
                                  and running away.
Someone found it bleeding, eating garbage
behind Safeway. What would you do
in this hard and hungry town? What husband, what wife? —
bound or terrorized by a lousy life.
What daughter crying in her room,
amber vial and a number?
What son without a song
snug to the muzzle
of a gun?

Brown Trout in Flood Grass

for David James Duncan

Yesterday's cows were rubbing fences
where today's spring river
rises, willow-combed, tree-tongued, swallowing

the oily low road and pump house,
covering field and pasture, spreading a wide shine,
waking wild trout

from their winter bed
to the flooded grass behind the sandbagged barn
and tractor. Gold bellied, brown spotted,

they part the grass and prey
over the land of cast hooks and sprayed poison,
the horrible thirst of wheat

that last summer sucked water low and burning.
Then came fall freshets, the cold faith of waiting,
and now these days and nights of answered rain

washing the used and dirty world
into worms and waxy grubs, ant eggs and sleeping spiders —
a deluge feast long promised the faithful.

V

At Any Cost

Why Men Want Women Naked

Because men really stare at things —
naked women, polished Corvettes,
deer in a meadow, house on fire, pizza arriving,
poker hands and a pile of cash.

Sure, there's truth behind the clouds.
What men make of themselves:
fiery sun, accomplished mountains,
lush glens and oceans swelled with urge.

Tonight in our room,
I only see by touching,
and ask with the glide of my palm.
Sometimes we leave a little light on,
but you say it shines away
the answers.

Cream on My Tail

This morning
I pour cream on the cat.
Just a little
down his black-striped
tabby
tail.

A goldfinch flies
through the open window,
circles the kitchen,
and thrums out
without
the cat
even noticing.

He turns back—licking, licking, licking.
Nice, he seems to say, glancing up.
Sweet,
rich,
really amazing—
Cream on my tail!

Business in Tahiti

After a steamed week of *Oui, Absolument,*
Pas de problème, I collapse
beside the hotel pool
where a mother and daughter
lounge topless.

    The woman takes off her sunglasses.
I put down my *Economist.* She lights
a cigarette, brunette hair pulled back
from her dark, shining chest.
The girl, maybe 14, gets into her robe.
They speak in French, pointing to the sky.
The girl walks away.
I check messages — snow back home,
daughter in a ditch, wife wondering how I'm doing.

    Doing? I say too loud.
A sudden breeze shifts the hibiscus,
dark clouds mass over Moorea.
The woman catches my gaze
and smiles. *Le tempête* arrive, I try to say.
I think so, she squints in English —
A storm would be exciting, non? she asks.

    Maybe, I say the first honest thing in weeks.
Peut-être, she smiles.

Osprey

Bandit eyes
cut the glare
to hover, plunge, hook and hold,
torpedo style,
the out-dazzled trout.
Pliny called you *Ossifraga,* Bone Breaker,
                              but it's flesh you rip
from the glistening twist.
High whistle, crook in the wing,
your crazy nest topping a tower.
Who would you call
if your mate,
fast to a big salmon, flapped and splashed,
                              pulled under the waves?
Osprey drowns, the birders blog.
It happens more than you'd think.
Moderation and restraint
evolving so slowly
in all of us.

Each Pocket Has a Chute

Loading iron ore on Lake Superior, Marquette, Michigan

On the ore dock
each pocket has a chute. A loader
brushes off his union suit
when the jennys from Empire skreak
and settle
high above the docking freighter.
The captain surveys
the sunny lake—two girls on jet skis
jumping a wake.
He's got one daughter in college, another in trouble,
and a son who games all day in sweats and stubble.
Sixty-six, and still not enough money.
The first mate lends him a twenty,
smiles into his radio and waves
to the loaders,
boot kicking doors for the noisy pour.
Another couple years, the captain thinks.
Another couple years, the first mate thinks.
                The girls glance up
then tail back
to the rusty beach
where their boyfriends
have just opened some wine—
expensive beyond their means—
thinking
it might make
a difference.

At the Woodburn Dragstrip

Revving,
smoke-scream burnout,
bit chomping roar
behind the *Christmas tree's* amber and green and —
                    Jesus, the noise —
          staring amazed
with my kids
     and a handful of bundled fans
in the rattling gray stands.

                         Times up on the board,
                    October's last swallows
turning clean white loops above the stained black strip.

Bannered under Pennzoil and Shell,
the National Guard recruits
from hood-popped humvees, handing us coupons
for corndogs. We eat and walk the quarter mile
to the finish line and a parked ambulance. Late season,
barely a soul. Rainclouds, grass fields,
gopher holes, a hovering hawk,
          and a supercharged yellow Chevelle
                    catching a silver Camaro at 160 miles-an-hour,
          parachuting down,
                    while the hawk wings over an old red barn.
Miles so open, so quietly grazed between heats,
you can feel us driving restless —
          even at four bucks a gallon —
somewhere far off the farm, suping-up the afternoon,
          dropping in
          a bigger engine of ourselves, horsepower
                         and blue blaze,
testing combustion
and alignment, reaction
and nerve. Power
and speed — straight ahead —
at any cost.

Ring-Necked Pheasant

They astound our flat fields with Chinese,
flash-cackle splash, exploding from high grass,
wild-winged and long tailed. Dogs bristle,
men swing to fire.

But here, for a moment, on a June green
with the coyote asleep and the hawk stuffed,
the pheasants open themselves to the sun,
preen their mottles, scratch and peck the seedy hill.

Tan-cheeked hens and a scarlet-wattled cock.
His raiment shimmers copper and gold,
the white-ringed throat tolls and tolls.

After Apples

One can see what will trouble
This sleep of mine
　　　　　　　　—Robert Frost

Dad's old truck
sprouting rust
and apple saplings
through the cracked skin
of the dash, the pull-choke
and springy hole
where I'd push in his lighter,
wait for the pop,
then pluck and guide
that burning blossom to his face
as we bumped along
to the buyer
with a load of hard apples.

When an October hurricane
blasted the orchard
we hauled trees and torn houses,
bedrooms and busted friends, driving exhausted
he said, *Gimme a light,*
then swerved from a rain-smeared phantom
and I burned his neck.
Goddamnit, he yelled. Then *Go on, light me up.*

The orchard's now an outlet mall,
and there's a hole in Dad's throat
I help clean. He buzzes my cloudy sleep
like that strange voice
at the McDonald's drive-thru

forty summers ago,
asking if we wanted apple pies.
Dad laughed and leaned out —*Sure. Make it two,*
splurging already
on cheeseburgers and large fries,
flushed with a few bucks
and sunny skies.

Release

The steelhead swallowed
the last flash of day —
head-shake, leap, and a fifty-foot peel
that raised the moon
in his reel. No one around.
No camera. Just three minutes,
a shaky net, unscaled
silver wild weight
thrashing.

Hook deep in the syrupy throat,
twist and thump, squeeze and needle nose fumble.

                                He would eat this fish,
but the law says
            let it go.
                                Gills puffing red,
he opens his hands and it bolts,
flutters, and floats, twenty feet away.

At camp, down river, his wife
strikes a lantern, puts on a jacket, and checks her watch.
There's a great slap
on the water's face
she marks and forgets,
wondering why he's so late.

Losing Leaves

People believed trees lost leaves
from exhaustion. Nine months
carrying sun and rain, birds and squirrels,
bug-worried and storm-stressed,
beavers at their knees.

But it's just hours of light in a day,
the sky-clock winding down to rest
when supplies dwindle and there's not much
left to do or say.

Yet that oak rattles brown leaves
all winter. And you won't throw away old magazines
or Christmas cards. Hanging on to boxes
of the kids' drawings and school work—

her long silent room.

Stuffed animals on wooden shelves,
dolls, books, those faded letters and posters falling
to the floor

should really be picked up now.
I know, Love, it's hard. I feel it, too. But it's time
to rake and bag it all. Not the letters,

of course,
but the rest.
I didn't say *dump*. I'm sorry.
Please, though. It's been two years.
And it's almost spring again.

Valentine's Day

Godiva heart
melting in traffic.
Home at seven to the cold house
where dark edges harden
back into what we know:
work first, love later. I toss
a nutty salad, then doze
on the couch with the cat.
You're home at nine
with red-ribboned wine
for a date we always keep
and pour, closing sleep
toward those years, we say,
when we'll wake with the whole day
to ourselves —
if we can, if we are.

VI

What's Left

What's Left

Home late from hunting,
a sauce splattered stove,
radio blaring, floor full of onions,
door wide open—something's not right—
the neighbor's collie licking
the sticky linoleum.
A couple hours late. What the fuck?
Empty bottle of wine, car gone,
messages blinking.
So he turns down the radio,
locks up his gun, pets the dog,
boils pasta, reheats sauce,
tears the bread, opens a new bottle
and sits down
to what's left.

My Fine Long Rod

These days
most of my nice slacks
are too tight. Belts out-notched,
briefs biting my waist,
jeans choking my crotch.
Having gained so much in the global market,
I celebrate with a feast — Beijing duck
and Shanghai dumplings, orange chicken
and a fortune cookie.
Swell wrapped
in the sweat suit of the mandarin,
I snooze on the bank,
laser sharpened hook
pressed with dough
at the end of a braided line.
Angled on a forked branch,
my fine long rod
of a style and quality
no longer made
in America.

A Horse and Bird History of Texas

Small equus grazing Texas
a few million years before Randy
roped his ranch. Before Sam Houston,
the Caddo, Comanche,
and big cats,
terror birds strutted up from the south
when the continents kissed. Terror birds—ten feet tall,
five hundred pounds, flightless, fast, ax billed—
chopping little Pleistocene ponies and themselves
into extinction.

Then nothing happened with horses
until Spanish brought their galloping jennets and Arabians,
their church, garlic and measles, leaving open the gate
for all of Europe. These days,
the biggest and bravest birds in Texas
sit on fence posts
and can only eat a horse that drops dead.
Not much glory in that, now,
is there, Tex?

Mola Mola,
Ocean Sunfish

Hey,
look!
Shark!
No, whale!
No wait, a Mola mola—
women scooping-up children, dogs
barking, young Johnny crazy for a catch.
We row out and see it bob and flop. Broad
and flat as a truck hood, moon-chinned, battered,
bearing the gray bulk of its long wandering,
       jellyfishing the trades, parasites, propellers
and plastic bags, slab tilting that scary dark dorsal,
people pointing and shouting, swimming nervously
                     away,
    though she's a sweet-mouthed, soft-eyed, big idea
      stumped with all our knowing. I splash her
cheek and that little fin, fluttering like a girl's fan
cooling down the blush of boys in the sun.
Let's tow it in, Johnny grins,
looping a black rope,
and muscling way over,
only to miss
and miss
her sinking
gray
brow.

Since the City Turned Blue

Down in New Orleans
for another church retreat
gone to hell in a night's drunken cheat.
I wake sick, pull out my rod, walk to the levee,
hook on a shrimp, cast and fall asleep.
Stirring between the stained grass and garbage,
horns, hammers and concrete resurrection—
somebody shouts *Hey!*
and I'm up fumbling, reeling. My rod bending crazy
wet wildness on a silvery run—
What the devil? I yell,
lifting the deep-bodied, grunting swish
up to the group of orange vested apostles.
Ain't no devil, says a guy from the crew—
*Just a gasper-goo. Get 'em all the time
since the city's turned blue.*

A Little Closer

Fishing for striped bass off Long Island, New York

Double hauling
downwind
you put me right on those stripers
driving baitfish insane against musseled rocks.
Stripping fast
through tern whirl and splash —
the oily chop moving off,
leaving my big white deceiver
swinging to the boat.

You put it in gear
to get me closer. A friend
even after
miles of arguments
and that Bridgeport backcast
that hooked your wife —
my two a.m. confession,
whisky-close at Danfords.

Closer.
Rolling a lead-eyed hackle
back in the riot
of mouth and tail. *Come on, take it!* I beg the fish,
then you, *Come on. A little closer.* Another cast.
Fish moving fast. Rocks under the hull.
That's enough, you hit reverse.
Please, I say. *Just a little closer.*

Sarcastic Fringehead

> *These West Coast fish live in shells and discarded*
> *bottles and sport some serious attitude.*
>
> —Milton S. Love

They bulldozed crusty tenements and trashy trailer courts.
Now the State's cleaning up those bottle fields off Redondo
where the tide chimes sweetly to glass and shell
and every longneck and flask flashes a fringehead
ensconced in slick sarcasm.

Thanks for the name, one burps at a glass-faced scientist,
while a redhead snaps *Nice manners* at a black-suited diver
grabbing her jugs. She may not be the prettiest fish—big-mouthed,
bug-eyed, that freaky stalk over the brow—
but watch her boyfriend's jealous jaws unhinge.

From a Jack bottle's broken neck,
the shoal's fattest fringehead shakes his head: *Really 'ppreciate*
cleaning up the environment an' all. Me and the old lady
are tired of washing windows anyway.
Maybe we'll move to Malibu.
Get a decanter in Paradise Cove.

Fishing Hungover

July
morning
hungover, alone,
rented rowboat
jigging —
sore neck, bruised knee,
last night
how?

Mouth raggy,
head aching,
no bites.

Standing
unzipped
to piss,

a loon pops up
billing a trout,
dripping,
swallowing,
blinking a curious red eye,

then diving
under my throbbing
astonished
happier
head.

Birds and Bluefin Tuna

Plunge
and rise,
shearwaters and tuna
feast together,
soft brown feathers and stiff blue fins,
dive and strike,
wing-stroking, scythe-tailing —
the anchovy ball
bouncing blood and scales —
chopsticks and rockets,
pinching, gulping, swallowing
flash
after bright flash,
swirling an ocean epitaph —
together, alive—
before the boats
and men
arrive.

VII

The Last Tool You'll Need

In a Voice Not a Child's

Aunt Lil
had an old Electrolux,
Just for sucking spiders,
she joked.
Big, scary spiders
inhaled from gauzy corners
and couched shadows
in our cozy rooms.

I can tell you
in a voice not a child's
that Lil smiled and laughed
with suited salesmen
brightened by her looks and charm,
but she never dated, never married.
She lived with us,
read romances
and kept things clean.

One afternoon,
concealed by the deafening
electric effort
and her own concentration,
I saw Lil put
the shiny sucking pipe
between her polyester thighs
and smile.

The Last Tool You'll Need

It must've been the discrete joys
of garden and shop,
greenhouse and garage
that kept the old couple happy
on the fixed income
of marriage.

Grandma's hook-billed
pruning shears
still screech to the squeeze.
Granddad's wood clamps
sigh unpressured. Tools say so much
about the way a person lived.
All their noise and silence,
trimming and joining,
shaping and fixing—for what?
The whole family thorned
and unglued
after their murky death.

Lunch, bills, grandkids, television.
A dusty vodka bottle down from cabinet,
orange juice and ice.
Their last three o'clock nap
sealed with pills
and the sweet kiss
of a screwdriver.

Man Killed While Playing Bigfoot, August 2012

Among all animals except humans,
apes take longest to mature.
                              —National Geographic

Flathead Lake, Montana,
a few beers and laughs between buddies.
Zip the suit. Okay, there's some headlights.
This is gonna be great.
          Step out on Highway 93,
                         lumber like an ape —
          Oh, shit.
          Not even a swerve.
          Smash and thump.
A fifteen-year-old girl
          runs him over.
What do you say
about Tater Tenley, 44, of Kalispell, Montana?
And how terrible for the girl driving the car,
for Tenley's son, Hunter,
and the beer-buying friend.

Someday, high in the jungles of Borneo,
an orangutan will put on a poacher's cap,
                    pick up some old netting
                              and leap
                              down
          on a busy branch,
          shit-scaring his shaggy friends
     bouncing and bellowing
          above the snaky loam.

Experiments with Rhesus Monkeys

I was chasing that rhesus monkey who slipped his cage
and ran around the lab, ate my Reese's Pieces,
and jerked-off on some files

when Dr. Shakespeare—his real name—walked in,
freaked, and spilled his milky coffee
on this $10,000 keyboard

custom made for monkeys to type. Twenty years of this
experiment and no *Hamlet*, believe me, but one
almost nailed Ashbery's "Dong"

in *stanzas shaped like banana boats,* I wrote in my notes,
and Shakespeare sneers, "What do banana boats
look like?" So I showed him.

Seeing the Greater Yellowlegs

Flock sprucing spring bogs,
north and north again.
Upturned bill and bobbing head,
she picks her life through shallows.

In a brightening Alaska meadow
a greater yellowlegs lowers her barred tail
and lays the last of her four buff eggs.

Her mate sounds alarm
as we walk up with iPhones
and capture the nest they flee,
immediately sending images
that prove to friends we see.

Making Islands

Tongues
brashing like dolphins,
we stroke
warm seams
and swells,
diving to the bed.

Depth can be scary—
twisted wrecks, whale bones,
dark rifts. But we want it, unzipping
into hot vents. Our luscious
cones swirl and blow,

and the island rises—
steam, smoke, fire and flow.
Glowing rivers
cooling shoulders
into sleep.

Over the years
love hardens, ripens,
and grows soft again. Gardens sway,
while our children play
in the warm sand,
then sail away
with people we hardly know.

Sun setting easy and rising slow,
we hope nothing
erupts or washes up
to be saved.
Rocks say we're sinking. That's okay.
The earth makes beautiful things
and takes them away.

Acknowledgements

Grateful acknowledgment is made to the editors of the following publications where many of these poems first appeared: *Adventures NW, Cloudbank, Hiram Poetry Review, Hubbub, Jefferson Monthly, Kentucky Review, Midwest Quarterly, Off the Coast, Owen Wister Review, Passages North, Prairie Winds, Rise Forms: Fly Fishing's Literary Voice, Shenandoah, Statesman Journal, Surrounded: Living with Islands, Timberline Review, Whitefish Review,* and *Windfall.*

"Action" received the 2012 Oscar Wilde Prize from Gival Press, Arlington, Virginia.

"Brown Trout in Flood Grass" appeared in *The Echoing Green: Poems of Fields, Meadows, and Grasses,* Everyman's Library Pocket Poets Series, edited by Cecily Parks.

"Oregon City Shad" received the 2014 Kenneth O. Hanson Award from *Hubbub,* Reed College, Portland, Oregon.

"Since the City Turned Blue" appeared in *Poems of the American South,* Everyman's Library Pocket Poets Series, edited by David Biespiel.